The Urbana Free Library

To renew: call 217-367-4057
or go to "*urbanafreelibrary.org*"
and select "Renew/Request Items"

Does it absorb or repel liquid?

Susan Hughes

Crabtree Publishing Company

www.crabtreebooks.com

What's the Matter?

Author: Susan Hughes
Publishing plan research and development:
   Reagan Miller
Project development: Clarity Content Services
Project management: Joanne Chan
Project coordinator: Kathy Middleton
Editors: Joanne Chan, Reagan Miller
Copy editor: Dimitra Chronopoulos
Proofreader: Kelly Spence, Kylie Korneluk
Design: Pixel Hive studio
Photo research: Linda Tanaka
Production coordinator and
   prepress technician: Tammy McGarr
Print coordinator: Margaret Amy Salter

Photographs:
Cover Shutterstock; p1 Dejan Ristovski/Shutterstock; p4 top Getty
Images/Thinkstock, mg7/Thinkstock; p5 Monkey Business
Images/Shutterstock; p6 Blinka/Shutterstock; p7 Anthony
Harris/Thinkstock; p8 George Doyle/Stockbyte/Thinkstock; p9
Corepics VOF/Shutterstock; p10 FreeBirdPhotos/Shutterstock; p11
Ivonne Wierink/Shutterstock; p12 smuay/Shutterstock; p13 left
ntstudio/Shutterstock, top right Ragnarock/Shutterstock, Quang
Ho/Shutterstock, Hurst Photo/Shutterstock; p14 asulov/Shutterstock;
p15 wasja/Shutterstock; p16 Dejan Ristovski/Shutterstock;
p17 left Aliaxei Shupeika/Thinkstock, Frans Rombout/Thinkstock;
p18 Chin Kit Sen/Shutterstock; p19 left Cathy Yeulet/Thinkstock,
Latsalomao/Thinkstock; p21 David Tanaka; p22 left yanugkelid/
Shutterstock, RusN/Thinkstock, Vadim Ponomarenko/Shutterstock.

Library and Archives Canada Cataloguing in Publication

Hughes, Susan, 1960-, author
      Does it absorb or repel liquid? / Susan Hughes.

(What's the matter)
Includes index.
Issued in print and electronic formats.
ISBN 978-0-7787-0537-6 (bound).--ISBN 978-0-7787-0541-3 (pbk.).--
ISBN 978-1-4271-9026-0 (html).--ISBN 978-1-4271-9030-7 (pdf)

      1. Hydrophobic surfaces--Juvenile literature. 2. Hydrophone--
Juvenile literature. 3. Matter--Properties--Juvenile literature. I. Title.
II. Series: What's the matter? (St. Catharines, Ont.)

QD509.S65H85 2014   j541'.335   C2014-900411-7
                                              C2014-900412-5

Library of Congress Cataloging-in-Publication Data

Hughes, Susan, 1960- author.
 Does it absorb or repel liquid? / Susan Hughes.
    pages cm. -- (What's the matter?)
 Audience: 5-8.
 Audience: K to grade 3.
 Includes index.
 ISBN 978-0-7787-0537-6 (reinforced library binding : alk. paper) -- ISBN 978-0-
7787-0541-3 (pbk. : alk. paper) -- ISBN 978-1-4271-9026-0 (electronic html) --
ISBN 978-1-4271-9030-7 (electronic pdf)
1. Surface tension--Juvenile literature. 2. Capillarity--Juvenile literature. 3.
Matter--Properties--Juvenile literature. I. Title.

QC183.H84 2014
530.4'27--dc23
                                       2014002260

Crabtree Publishing Company

www.crabtreebooks.com   1-800-387-7650

Printed in Canada/032014/MA20140124

Published in Canada
Crabtree Publishing
616 Welland Ave.
St. Catharines, ON
L2M 5V6

Published in the United States
Crabtree Publishing
PMB 59051
350 Fifth Avenue, 59th Floor
New York, New York 10118

Published in the United Kingdom
Crabtree Publishing
Maritime House
Basin Road North, Hove
BN41 1WR

Published in Australia
Crabtree Publishing
3 Charles Street
Coburg North
VIC 3058

What is in this book?

What is matter?

All objects are made of **matter**.

Matter takes up space.

Matter has **mass**.

Mass is the amount of material in an object.

You are made of matter, too!

What are properties?

Matter has **properties**.

Properties describe how something looks, feels, tastes, smells, or sounds.

We can hear if something is loud or soft.

We can see if something **absorbs**, or soaks up, water or if it does not.

Absorbency is when an object soaks up water. Absorbency is a property of matter, too.

Does it absorb liquid?

Some objects absorb **liquids**, such as water, juice, or oil.

We use a towel to dry our bodies after swimming.

8

A mechanic uses a cloth to clean his hands.

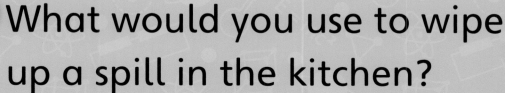

What would you use to wipe up a spill in the kitchen?

Does it repel liquid?

Some objects do not absorb liquid. They **repel** it. Things that repel water are called **waterproof**.

A raincoat repels liquids.

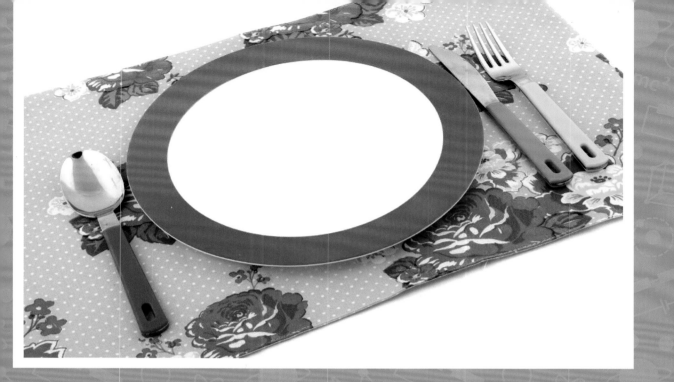

Some place mats repel liquids.
You can wipe them clean.

What do you wear on your feet when it rains? Do they absorb or repel water?

Is it porous?

Most materials that absorb liquids are **porous**.

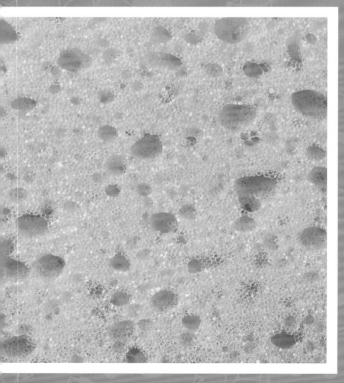

Porous materials have tiny openings in them. The openings let in liquid.

A sponge is porous. It absorbs liquid.

Rubber is not porous. Rubber tires do not absorb water.

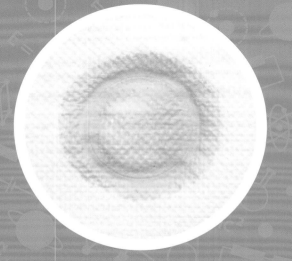

Paper is porous. It absorbs liquid.

On a rainy day, would you carry your lunch in a plastic or a paper bag? Why?

Soak it up!

Objects change when they absorb water.

Some get heavier.

Put a dry towel in the washing machine. When it is clean, lift it out. Was it heavier when it was wet or dry?

Some objects get bigger when they absorb water.

Have you ever dropped a book in water? The pages soak up water. So does the cover.

Now the book cannot close properly!

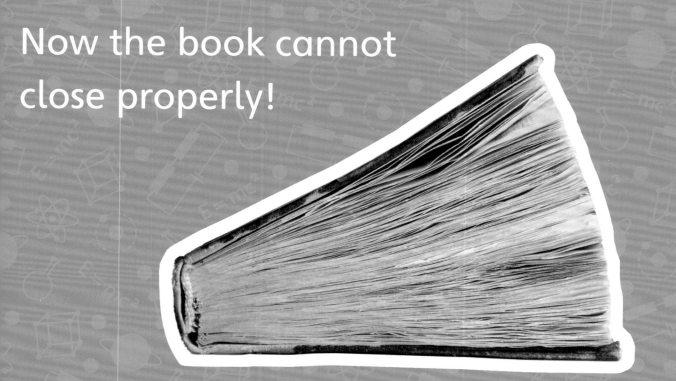

Objects that absorb liquid

Objects that absorb liquid help us in many ways.

We use them to clean up where we work and live.

We use them to keep our bodies clean.

We use them to dry off.

Objects that repel liquid

Waterproof objects repel liquids. They protect us from getting wet. They protect many things from getting wet!

They also protect things from being ruined.

A waterproof jacket keeps a dog dry.

A plastic apron protects clothes from spills.

A duck's body makes oil. Oil repels water. The oil is on the duck's feathers. How do waterproof feathers help ducks?

Suck it up!

Which objects absorb water? Which do not?

Find small objects. You can use coins, buttons, candies, raisins, cotton balls, and seeds. Put them in water. Leave them for a day.

Are they different now?

Are they heavier?

Are they bigger?

What happens when you squeeze them?

Which clues helped you decide if the object absorbs or repels water?

Absorb or repel?

Use what you have learned from this book to tell which object in each picture absorbs liquids and which repels liquids.

A

B

C

Answer:
A) Rubber gloves repel water. A sponge absorbs water.
B) Soil absorbs water.
C) A mop absorbs water.

22

Words to know and Index

absorb
pages
7–17

liquids
pages
8–13, 16, 18

mass
page 4

matter
pages
4–6

properties
pages 6-7

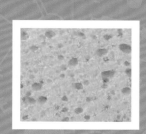

porous
pages
12–13

repel
pages
10–11,
18–19

waterproof
pages 10,
18–19

Notes for adults

Objectives

- to introduce children to the difference between objects that absorb liquids and objects that repel liquids
- to learn about how people use these objects in everyday life

Prerequisite

Ask the children to read *Does it sink or float?* before reading *Does it absorb or repel liquid?* Introducing them to the concepts of sinking and floating with *Does it sink or float?* will help familiarize them with the initial concepts in this book.

Questions before reading *Does it absorb or repel liquid?*

"Tell me about a time when you put something in water and it soaked the water up."

"How is something that soaks up water different from something that does not?"

"When would you ever use something that does not soak up water?"

Discussion

Read the book with the children. Discuss with the children some of the main words and concepts in the book, such as absorb and repel, liquids, absorbency, and porous.

Have the children use markers to draw a row of dots in different colors at one end of a paper towel. Tell them they will dip the other end of the paper towel in water, and ask them to predict what will happen. Have them do the experiment and observe how the water is absorbed. Ask them to describe what they see.

Extension

Have the children draw with wax crayons on paper. Have them paint over the paper with watercolor paint in different colors. Ask them to describe what they see, using the words "absorb" and "repel." (The wax in the crayon will repel the water; the paper will absorb it.)